ChatGPT Catalyst: Student Edition

First published in 2025 by CorePrint
An independent publication
Typeset in Playfair Display & Lato

This publication is independently distributed via CorePrint, Amazon KDP, Gumroad, and Etsy in PDF and print formats. It is not affiliated with, endorsed by, or sponsored by OpenAI or any related entity.

Contents

Part One: 📚 Study Help

Contents

Part Two: ✍️ Writing

Part Three: ⏳ Time Management

Contents

Contents

Welcome To ChatGPT Catalyst: Student Edition

Whether you're writing an essay the night before it's due, juggling part-time work with a full study load, or just trying to stay motivated, this guide is built for you.

ChatGPT is one of the most powerful tools available to students today. But knowing how to ask the right questions makes all the difference. This book gives you carefully crafted prompts that unlock ChatGPT's full potential, so you can stop feeling overwhelmed and start working smarter.

Each prompt in this guide is designed with real student struggles in mind. You'll find help with study routines, time management, writing support, and more—each one tested and structured to deliver efficient, relevant responses from ChatGPT.

By learning these prompts, you will:

- Save time when researching, writing, and planning.
- Communicate more clearly in assignments and projects.
- Get unstuck faster with tailored support.
- Improve your academic workflow using AI.

How To Use This Book

This guide was built to make ChatGPT simple, powerful, and useful — even for those who have never used a prompt in their lives.

Each page contains one carefully crafted prompt designed for students. You'll find study tools, writing support, time-saving tips, and mindset boosters — all categorised by topic and difficulty.

What each section means:

- 🧠 **Prompt:**
    - The exact phrase to copy or customize in ChatGPT.
- 💡 **Ideal Use:**
    - When to use it, and what kind of problem it solves.
- 🤖 **Sample Output:**
    - A short preview of what ChatGPT might return.
- 📌 **Quick Tip:**
    - A bonus suggestion to help you refine or extend the result.

How to get the best results:

- Start with Beginner prompts if you're new to ChatGPT.
- Modify prompts by adding your own subject, deadline, or task.
- Combine multiple prompts for layered tasks (e.g. writing + editing).
- Don't be afraid to ask ChatGPT to revise or rephrase until it's just right.

Part 1
Study Help

Prompts designed to help you learn faster, retain more, and tackle your study sessions with clarity

Beginner 🟢
Prompt: *"Explain [**specific concept**] to me like I'm 5 years old, using simple words and examples."*

Use case: Quickly grasp a difficult concept by having it broken down into super simple terms.

Sample Output: *"[**Concept**] is like a [**very simple analogy**]. Imagine... (ChatGPT continues with a basic, child-friendly explanation in 1–3 sentences)."*

Tip: Follow up by asking for a slightly more detailed explanation or a real-world example once you understand the basics.

Beginner 🟢
Prompt: "Summarise the key points of [**text or topic**] in a concise, bullet-point list."

Use case: Get the main ideas from a textbook chapter, article, or lecture notes without wading through all the details.

Sample Output: "• Point 1:... • Point 2:... • Point 3:..." (ChatGPT provides a brief list of the most important points.)

Tip: If the summary misses something you need, ask ChatGPT to elaborate on that point or provide more context.

Intermediate 🟡
Prompt: *"Give me a memorable analogy or story to help me understand [**difficult concept**]."*

Use case: Learn complex ideas by linking them to familiar situations or fun stories, making them easier to remember.

Sample Output: *"Understanding [**concept**] is kind of like [**analogy**]. Imagine ..."* (ChatGPT then tells a short analogy or story in 2–3 sentences that parallels the concept.)

Tip: After hearing the analogy, explain the concept back to ChatGPT in your own words or ask for another analogy if you need a different perspective.

Intermediate 🟡
Prompt: *"Show me how to apply [**concept**] with a step-by-step example problem (and explain each step simply)."*

Use case: See exactly how to use a formula or concept in practice by walking through an example problem with explanations at each step.

Sample Output: *"Problem:... Step 1: First, we... (because...) Step 2: Next, we..."* (ChatGPT demonstrates solving the problem, explaining the reason behind each step in simple terms.)

Tip: Try solving a similar problem on your own, then use ChatGPT to check your work or to clarify any steps you found confusing.

Intermediate 🟡

Prompt: *"Help me remember [**list of facts or terms**] by creating a catchy mnemonic or phrase."*

Use case: Memorize tough facts, formulas, or sequences using a fun acronym, rhyme, or phrase that sticks in your mind.

Sample Output: *"**To remember the** [**X elements or steps**], **think:** '[**Funny or catchy sentence where each word starts with the needed letters**].'"*

Tip: If the first mnemonic isn't clicking for you, ask ChatGPT for a different one or to explain the logic behind it so you can tweak it yourself.

Intermediate 🟡

Prompt: *"What are the top 3 most important concepts in [**topic**], and why are they important?"*

Use case: Focus your studying on the high-impact ideas that give you the biggest understanding payoff (the 80/20 rule of learning).

Sample Output: *"**1. Key Concept A:** This is crucial because... **2. Key Concept B:**... **3. Key Concept C:**..."* (ChatGPT lists three major concepts and briefly explains their significance.)

Tip: Use this as a starting point—once you know the key concepts, you can ask ChatGPT for resources or examples for each one to deepen your understanding.

Intermediate 🟡

Prompt: *"I have an exam on [**subject**] in 2 weeks. Create a daily study plan covering all the important topics, with review days and breaks included."*

Use case: Get a realistic, stress-free study schedule that tells you what to study each day and when to rest, so you're fully prepared by exam day.

Sample Output: *"**Study Plan: Day 1** – Review Chapter 1 basics; **Day 2** – Practice problems on Topic X;... **Day 5** – Rest or light review;... **Day 14** – Final review of key points."* (ChatGPT outlines a day-by-day plan in 1–3 sentences.)

Tip: After getting the plan, tell ChatGPT which topics you find hardest or if you miss a study day, and ask it to adjust the schedule accordingly.

Intermediate 🟡

Prompt: *"Quiz me on [**topic**] with 5 challenging questions, and then provide the correct answers and explain them."*

Use case: Test your knowledge with practice questions generated on the fly, then immediately check your answers and learn from the explanations.

Sample Output: *"**Q1**:...? **A1**:... (Explanation: ...) **Q2**:...? **A2**:... (**Explanation:...**)"* (ChatGPT lists questions followed by their answers and brief explanations.)

Tip: Try answering each question on your own before looking at ChatGPT's answer. If you get one wrong, ask for more clarification or another question on that sub-topic.

Advanced 🔴

Prompt: *"Act as a diagnostic tutor for [**topic**]. First, ask me 3 quick questions of varying difficulty to assess my understanding. After I answer (**I will type my answers**), identify my weak areas and suggest specific resources or tips to improve."*

Use case: Pinpoint exactly what you don't know about a subject and get targeted advice on fixing those gaps, almost like a personal tutor would do.

Sample Output: "***Question 1:****...?* ***Question 2:****...?* ***Question 3:****...?* * (After your answers, ChatGPT responds)* *It looks like you've mastered A and B, but you struggled with C. I recommend reviewing Chapter 3 on C or watching a tutorial on [**C**], then practicing related problems."*

Tip: Be honest with your answers. After ChatGPT's feedback, you can ask it to explain the specific weak area (**C in this case**) in a different way or provide practice questions just on that part.

Intermediate 🟡

Prompt: *"Compare and contrast [**Concept A**] and [**Concept B**] in simple terms, and give an example of how each is used."*

Use case: Clear up confusion between two similar concepts by seeing them side-by-side, including a real example to illustrate the differences.

Sample Output: *"**Concept A vs. Concept B:** Concept A is... whereas Concept B is... **Example:** A is like... in scenario X, but B is like... in scenario Y."*

Tip: If you're still unsure, ask ChatGPT to make a quick table of differences or to use a different analogy for the comparison.

Beginner 🟢

Prompt: *"What are common mistakes students make with [**topic or problem**], and how can I avoid them?"*

Use case: Learn from others' mistakes – find out typical pitfalls or misconceptions in a topic so you can sidestep them on homework and exams.

Sample Output: *"**Common mistakes in [topic] include:** 1) Misinterpreting… (Avoid this by…), 2) Forgetting to… (Remember to…)."*

Tip: After reading the list, double-check your own understanding by explaining to ChatGPT why each mistake is wrong. You can even take a problem you solved and ask if you fell into any of those traps.

Beginner 🟢

Prompt: *"Explain why [**topic**] actually matters in real life – how is it used or why is it important?"*

Use case: Boost your motivation (and understanding) by seeing the real-world relevance of what you're learning, turning abstract topics into something meaningful.

Sample Output: *"[**Topic**] is important because... For example, in real life it's used to [**application**], which helps [**who/how**]."*

Tip: Use this real-life connection as a memory hook. Later on, if you get stuck on the topic, recalling the practical example can help reinforce your understanding.

Intermediate 🟡

Prompt: *"**Here are my notes on [topic]: [paste bullet-point notes**]. Organize these into a clear, concise cheat-sheet or study guide for quick review."*

Use case: Turn messy or lengthy notes into a well-organized summary, so you have a clean cheat-sheet to review before a test.

Sample Output: *"**Topic:**... - **Key Definition:**... - **Formula:**... - **Example:**..."* (ChatGPT restructures and condenses your notes into study-friendly bullet points or sections.)

Tip: If the output is still too long, ask ChatGPT to condense it further or highlight the absolutely must-know points in bold. You can also request it in a certain format (e.g., a table, Q&A flashcard style, etc.).

Beginner 🟢

Prompt: *"Break down the process of [**complex process or mechanism**] into a few simple steps I can easily follow."*

Use case: Understand a complex process (scientific, mathematical, or procedural) by seeing it in a step-by-step format, almost like a mini flowchart described in words.

Sample Output: *"**Process:** 1) First, [**Step 1 in simple terms**]. 2) Then, [**Step 2**]... 3) Next, [**Step 3**]... 4) Finally, [**Step 4**]."*

Tip: After reading the steps, try to explain them back without looking. If you struggle with a step, ask ChatGPT to clarify that step further or explain why it's done.

Intermediate 🟡

Prompt: *"I keep getting stuck on [**type of problem**]. Walk me through an example problem step-by-step, explaining why each step makes sense."*

Use case: If there's a kind of problem that always trips you up (like a tricky math proof or a certain grammar exercise), have ChatGPT demonstrate solving one in detail so you can follow the logic.

Sample Output: *"**Let's solve this problem:... Step 1:** We do... because... **Step 2:*** Next... *(this works because...)* ***Step 3:** Then..."* (and so on, with clear reasoning).

Tip: Once you've seen the example, try a similar problem and explain your reasoning to ChatGPT. You can even ask, *"Did I do this right?"* and paste your solution for feedback.

Advanced 🔴

Prompt: *"I want to remember [**topic**] long-term. Give me a review schedule using spaced repetition over the next month (**when should I revisit the material, and what should I review each time?**)."*

Use case: Solidify your learning by following an AI-generated spaced repetition plan – it will tell you when and what to review (e.g., after 1 day, 3 days, 1 week, etc.) so you don't forget the material.

Sample Output: *"**Spaced Repetition Plan: Review 1:** Tomorrow – re-read notes and quiz yourself on basics. **Review 2:** 3 days later – do practice problems on key points. **Review 3:** one week later –… **Review 4:** two weeks later –… **Review 5:** one month later – final recap."*

Tip: Set calendar reminders for these review sessions. You can also ask ChatGPT to generate some quick questions for each review session when the time comes, to test what you remember.

Beginner 🟢
Prompt: *"Create 5 flashcard-style Q&A pairs to help me review [**topic**] (**questions on one side, answers on the other**)."*

Use case: Get a quick set of flashcards generated for quick-fire review – you can quiz yourself with the questions and then check against the answers.

Sample Output: *"**Q1:** What is...? **A1:** It is... **Q2:** How does...? **A2:** By ..."* (ChatGPT provides a list of question-answer pairs on the topic.)

Tip: Hide the answers and try to answer each question first. If you get any wrong, ask ChatGPT to give a hint for that question, or to explain the answer in a different way so you understand it better.

Advanced 🔴

Prompt: *"Help me explain [**topic**] to someone else (**like a study buddy**) in simple terms. Provide a brief script or outline I could use to teach it."*

Use case: One of the best ways to learn is to teach. This prompt prepares you to teach a friend by giving you a mini lesson-plan or script, which in turn reinforces your own understanding.

Sample Output: *"**Teaching Outline: 1.** Start by defining [**topic**] in one sentence... **2.** Use a simple example: 'Imagine...' **3.** Check understanding by asking: 'What if...?' **4.** Summarise the key point:..."*

Tip: Actually try teaching the concept using this outline (even if just to an imaginary friend or a rubber duck!). If you get stuck during the explanation, note where, and ask ChatGPT to help clarify that part further.

Intermediate 🟡

Prompt: *"**Make learning [topic] fun:** explain it with a bit of humour or a goofy story so it keeps me engaged."*

Use case: Keep boredom at bay by having ChatGPT inject some humour into the learning process – a funny analogy or silly story can make studying more enjoyable and memorable.

Sample Output: *"[**Topic**] might seem dull, but imagine if it were a [**silly scenario**]…"* (ChatGPT then gives a playful, humorous explanation or story in 2–3 sentences that still teaches the concept.)

Tip: Don't hesitate to ask for the same explanation in a different comedic style if it helps (for example, *"Explain it like a stand-up comedian would"* or *"Give me a pun about it"*). Laughter can actually help you remember the info!

Advanced 🔴

Prompt: *"Challenge me with a tough question on [**topic**] to test deep understanding, then reveal the answer with an explanation I can learn from."*

Use case: After you think you've mastered a topic, use this to push your understanding to the limit. A hard, thought-provoking question ensures you're truly exam-ready, and the explained answer helps fill any last gaps.

Sample Output: *"**Challenge Question:...**? (**This question is tricky because...**) **Answer:**..., **Explanation:**..."* (ChatGPT poses a difficult problem, then provides a thorough solution and explanation.)

Tip: Treat it like a real test: try to solve the challenge question on your own first. If you get it right, great! If not, study the explanation carefully and ask follow-up questions on any part of the solution you still don't understand.

Part 2
Writing

Use these prompts to improve your writing, from generating ideas and outlines to refining your drafts and practicing creative writing.

Beginner 🟢
Prompt: *"I need to write about [**broad topic**]. Can you help me brainstorm a list of creative or interesting ideas/subtopics to write about?"*

Use case: Kick-start an assignment with a list of potential angles or subtopics so you're not staring at a blank page.

Sample Output: *"Sure! For [**broad topic**], **you could explore:** 1) Idea A –... 2) Idea B –... 3) Idea C –..."* (ChatGPT lists a few unique ideas, each briefly explained in one sentence.)

Tip: If none of the ideas excite you, tell ChatGPT which parts you like or dislike about the suggestions, and ask for more ideas based on your preferences.

Beginner 🟢
Prompt: *"Help me outline an essay on [**your essay topic**]. I need a solid thesis statement and main points for each paragraph."*

Use case: Quickly get a structured game plan for your essay – a thesis to guide you and an outline of what each paragraph will cover.

Sample Output: *"**Thesis:** [**Clear argument or stance**]. **Outline:** I. Introduction – introduce topic and thesis. II. **Point 1:**... III. **Point 2:**... IV. **Point 3:**... V. Conclusion – wrap up and restate thesis."*

Tip: Use the generated outline as a starting point. You can ask ChatGPT to expand any section of the outline into a paragraph or to provide examples for a specific point if you get stuck while writing.

Intermediate

Prompt: *"I have a basic thesis: [**your thesis**]. How can I make this thesis statement stronger or more specific?"*

Use case: Refine a weak or generic thesis into a compelling argument that gives your essay a clear direction and originality.

Sample Output: *"Your thesis is a good start. You could sharpen it like this: [**Improved thesis version**], because it [**reason why it's stronger**]."*

Tip: Once you have the improved thesis, ask ChatGPT for a quick outline or for evidence that would support that thesis, to ensure you can actually back it up in your essay.

Intermediate

Prompt: *"Give me 3 possible catchy titles for an essay about [**topic**], and explain the tone each title sets."*

Use case: Find an attention-grabbing title for your paper or article and understand how different titles might come across to your reader.

Sample Output: *"1) "[**Title 1**]" – this sounds analytical and serious.*
*2) "[**Title 2**]" – this one is playful and grabs attention by...*
*3) "[**Title 3**]" – this title is straightforward and informative..."*

Tip: If none of the titles feel perfect, mix and match phrases or ask ChatGPT to combine a certain style from one with an element from another. You can also ask for more titles in a specific tone (e.g., humorous, academic, dramatic).

Beginner 🟢

Prompt: *"Proofread the following text for grammar, spelling, and clarity, and then show me the corrected version: "[**your sentence or paragraph**]"."*

Use case: Instantly fix grammar and spelling mistakes in your writing and see a cleaner, clearer version of your sentence/paragraph.

Sample Output: *"**Original:** [**Your text**] **Revised:** [**Your text with corrections**]"* (ChatGPT outputs your text with all errors corrected and wording improved for clarity.)

Tip: To learn from the corrections, ask ChatGPT to briefly explain why it changed certain phrases or punctuation. This way, you'll avoid repeating those mistakes in the future.

Beginner

Prompt: *"Rewrite this sentence/paragraph to make it clearer and easier to understand: "[**your confusing or wordy sentence**]"."*

Use case: Turn long, awkward, or confusing sentences into crisp, clear ones that any reader can follow. Great for polishing your essays or reports.

Sample Output: *"**Original:** It is the case that in many situations... **Rewritten:** Often, ..."* (ChatGPT provides a more straightforward version of your sentence or paragraph.)

Tip: If the rewritten version changes the tone or isn't what you intended, tell ChatGPT what you were aiming for (e.g., more formal, or simpler, or more concise) and ask it to try again with that in mind.

Intermediate 🟡

Prompt: *"I have a very short paragraph about [**topic**]. Can you expand it by adding more detail and examples while keeping it relevant?"*

Use case: Take a skimpy paragraph and enrich it with additional content—explanations, examples, or facts—to meet a word count or add depth to your argument.

Sample Output: *"Sure.* ***Original:*** *[**Your short paragraph**]* ***Expanded:*** *[**New longer paragraph**]* (ChatGPT adds explanations, an example or two, and perhaps an extra sentence to drive the point home.)"

Tip: If the expanded paragraph includes facts or claims, be sure to double-check their accuracy. You can also ask ChatGPT to focus the expansion in a certain way, like *"add a historical example"* or *"include a statistic if possible."*

Intermediate 🟡

Prompt: *"I need to cut down my word count. Condense the following text to about [**X**] words without losing any important information: "[**your long passage**]"."*

Use case: Trim verbose writing down to the essentials – perfect for meeting a word limit on assignments while keeping all the key points.

Sample Output: *"Condensed (≈**X words**): [**Shortened version of your text**]"* (ChatGPT rewrites your passage more succinctly, maintaining the main ideas.)

Tip: After you get the condensed version, verify that every crucial point is still there. If something important is missing, let ChatGPT know what must stay, or ask it to condense less aggressively.

Intermediate

Prompt: *"Change the tone of this passage to be more [**desired tone: formal, casual, persuasive, etc.**]: "[**your passage**]"."*

Use case: Instantly adjust the style of your writing – make an overly casual piece sound formal and academic, or make a dry piece more relatable – depending on your audience.

Sample Output: *"Revised in a more formal tone: [**Your passage rewritten with formal vocabulary and structure**]."*

Tip: You can combine this with other requests. For example, *"Make it more formal and add a transitional sentence between these two ideas."* The more specific you are about the tone or style, the better ChatGPT can tailor the text.

Intermediate

Prompt: *"Improve the flow of this paragraph. It feels choppy/disconnected: "[**your paragraph**]". Add transitions or rearrange if needed."*

Use case: Get help making your paragraph read smoothly. ChatGPT will add linking words and possibly reorganize sentences so ideas connect logically.

Sample Output: *"Revised Paragraph: [**Your paragraph with added transition phrases and a clearer logical order**]."*

Tip: If one part of the paragraph still seems abrupt, ask a follow-up like, *"Can you add a transition after this sentence to introduce the next idea?"* This way, you fine-tune the flow to perfection.

Advanced 🔴

Prompt: *"Here's my argument [**briefly describe your argument**]. Can you spot any weak points or logical gaps in it and suggest how to address them?"*

Use case: Strengthen your argument by having ChatGPT critique it. It will find places where your reasoning might be shaky or unsupported and tell you how to improve.

Sample Output: *"One potential weak point is [**point**], because... You could address this by [**suggestion, e.g., providing evidence or clarifying assumptions**]. Another gap is..."*

Tip: Use this feedback to revise your argument or essay. You can even ask ChatGPT to help find evidence or examples for the suggested fixes, or to rephrase a claim to be more accurate.

Intermediate 🟡

Prompt: *"I'm trying to support the idea that [**your point**]. Suggest a hypothetical example or scenario that illustrates this point well."*

Use case: Enrich your writing with concrete examples. ChatGPT will generate a believable scenario or anecdote that makes your point more convincing to the reader.

Sample Output: *"For instance, imagine [**scenario**]. In this situation, [**your point**] becomes clear because..."*

Tip: After getting the example, you can ask for additional types of support, like a statistic or a quotation, but be careful—ChatGPT might make up stats or quotes. Always verify any factual details it provides, or just use them as placeholders to research later.

Advanced 🔴

Prompt: *"Give me two strong counterarguments to my thesis [**briefly state thesis**], and how I might refute each one."*

Use case: Prepare for a debate or strengthen an argumentative essay by understanding the other side's best points – and figuring out how to argue against them.

Sample Output: *"**Counterargument 1:** Some might say... **Refutation:** However,... (explain why your stance still holds). **Counterargument 2:** Another argument is... **Refutation:** On the contrary,..."*

Tip: Use these counterarguments in your essay to show you've considered multiple perspectives. If ChatGPT's refutations feel weak, ask it to elaborate or to find evidence supporting your refutation.

Advanced 🔴

Prompt: *"Act as an English teacher. Evaluate the clarity and effectiveness of this paragraph and give specific suggestions for improvement: "[**your paragraph**]"."*

Use case: Get constructive criticism on your writing as if a teacher or editor were reviewing it. ChatGPT will point out what's good and what could be better, and how to improve it.

Sample Output: *"**Feedback:** The paragraph is clear in intent but could be more concise. For example, the sentence '...' is a bit confusing; you might split it into two. Also, consider varying your sentence starters. Overall, adding an example would strengthen your point about X."*

Tip: After receiving feedback, you can ask ChatGPT to implement the suggestions (e.g., *"Can you show me how the revised paragraph would look with those changes?"*). This way, you see the actual improvements in context.

Intermediate

Prompt: *"I need to write a cover letter for a [**position**] internship at [**company/type of company**]. Help me draft a compelling opening paragraph that highlights my enthusiasm and one relevant achievement."*

Use case: Save time on professional writing. ChatGPT will formulate a strong, positive opening for your cover letter, which you can then customize and build upon.

Sample Output: *"Dear Hiring Manager, I am excited to apply for the [**Position**] internship at [**Company**]. As a [**your role/major**] who [notable achievement or experience], I have developed [**skill or quality**] that I'm eager to bring to your team. ..."*

Tip: Use the output as a template. Then ask ChatGPT for help with other parts of the letter, like a closing paragraph or how to talk about another specific experience, to ensure your whole letter is cohesive and targeted.

Intermediate

Prompt: *"I'm working on my personal statement for a college application. I want to write about [**life experience or theme**]. Can you help me outline a narrative flow for it with a clear beginning, middle, and end that highlights personal growth?"*

Use case: Structure a compelling personal story for applications by outlining how to start (the hook or initial situation), what to include in the middle (challenges, learning experiences), and how to conclude (reflecting on growth or future goals).

Sample Output: *"**Outline:...** **Beginning:** Describe [**initial situation or challenge**] and how you felt. **Middle:** Narrate the turning point when [**what you did or learned**]. Include specific example of [**challenge**]. **End:** Reflect on how this experience changed you - what skills or perspective you gained, and how it leads you to [**college or future aspirations**]."*

Tip: Once you have the outline, draft the actual paragraphs and then use ChatGPT to refine them. For example, you can say *"Here's my draft intro based on that outline – any suggestions to make it more engaging?"*

Intermediate 🟡

Prompt: *"Turn this simple description into a vivid, detailed scene: "[**e.g. It was a sunny day in the park and I studied under a tree**]"."*

Use case: Enhance creative pieces or narrative essays with richer imagery. ChatGPT will transform basic descriptions into more evocative prose full of sensory details.

Sample Output: *"The sun spilled warmth over the busy park, where I sat beneath a towering oak. Golden light flickered through the leaves onto my textbook as a soft breeze turned the pages for me. In the background, children's laughter mixed with the rustle of papers spread around me, turning an ordinary study session into a moment of peace."*

Tip: If the style isn't quite what you want, you can ask for adjustments. For example, *"Can you make it even more descriptive of the surroundings?"* or *"Tone down the flowery language just a bit."* This helps match the scene to your personal writing voice.

Intermediate

Prompt: *"I'm stuck in my story.* ***I've written: [brief excerpt of your story]****. Can you suggest what might happen next, or give me a few ideas for the next scene?"*

Use case: Overcome writer's block in creative writing by having ChatGPT propose possible continuations or twists for your story based on what's happened so far.

Sample Output: *"Maybe [****Character****] discovers [****surprising event****], which leads to [****next conflict****]. For instance, in the next scene, you could have them..."* (ChatGPT gives one or two plausible directions with a sentence or two of explanation for each.)

Tip: You can specify the style or outcome you're looking for (e.g., *"I want a happy twist"* or *"Looking for something dramatic"*). Also, once you choose an idea, ask ChatGPT to help flesh it out further, like writing a quick paragraph of that scene to get you started.

Beginner

Prompt: *"I need a strong concluding paragraph for my essay about [**topic**]. Can you write a conclusion that summarises the main points and leaves a lasting impression?"*

Use case: End your essay on a high note. ChatGPT will produce a concise summary of your argument with a final thought or call-back that makes your essay feel complete and impactful.

Sample Output: *"In conclusion, [**restate thesis in new words**]. As explored, [**Point 1**], [**Point 2**], and [**Point 3**] all demonstrate that [**final insight**]. Recognizing this [**topic's significance or call to action**] is crucial, not just on paper, but in practice."*

Tip: Provide ChatGPT with the main points you want to include if possible (either in the prompt or by following up with your draft summary) for a more tailored conclusion. After getting the conclusion, ensure it doesn't introduce any new information – it should only wrap up what you've already discussed.

Beginner

Prompt: *"Write a short poem or haiku about [**subject or emotion**]."*

Use case: Have a bit of fun with words or fulfil a creative assignment by letting ChatGPT generate poetry. Whether it's a serious subject or just for laughs, this can give you a quick burst of creative text.

Sample Output: *"Books spread on the desk, Midnight oil fuels eager eyes, Dreams dawn in margins."* (**A simple haiku about studying, for example.**)

Tip: Use the generated poem as inspiration. If it's a class assignment, you might tweak the lines or structure. You can also ask for different forms (like a sonnet, limerick, free verse) or for the poem to convey a certain tone (hopeful, melancholy, etc.) to suit your needs.

Part 3
Time Management

Use these prompts to organize your schedule, fight procrastination, and make the most of your study time and personal time.

Beginner

Prompt: *"I have a lot to do. Help me prioritize and plan my day. My tasks are: [**list tasks**]."*

Use case: Get a clear, prioritized to-do list for the day so you tackle the most important things first and don't feel overwhelmed.

Sample Output: *"**Plan for Today: 1)** [**Most urgent task**] – do this first because... **2)** [**Next task**] – then this, since... **3)** [**Task**] – can wait until afternoon. Try to finish Task 1 by noon, then take a short break."*

Tip: Let ChatGPT know if you have deadlines or specific time constraints for each task; it can then organize your day more effectively. You can also ask it to allocate rough time blocks (e.g., 9–10am for Task 1) if you want a timed schedule.

Beginner

Prompt: *"Create a weekly study schedule for me. I have classes in the mornings and want to study [**subjects**] in the afternoons/evenings, plus some downtime on the weekend."*

Use case: Lay out a balanced weekly routine that slots in study sessions for each subject, along with class times and necessary breaks or leisure time.

Sample Output: *"**Weekly Schedule: Monday:** Class 9–12; **2–4pm** - Math review; **4–5pm** break/gym. **Tuesday:** Class 10–12; **2–5pm** - Chemistry homework; Evening free.... **Sunday:** Day off or light review of tough topics."*

Tip: Provide any specific commitments (club meetings, work hours, family time) to ChatGPT so it can factor those in. After you get the schedule, you can ask it to adjust if something doesn't fit (e.g., *"I actually work Thursday evenings, can you redo Thursday?"*).

Intermediate

Prompt: *"I have a big project due in a month. Break it down into smaller tasks with deadlines each week so I don't leave it all until the end."*

Use case: Avoid last-minute panic by having ChatGPT split a long-term project or assignment into bite-sized tasks, each with its own mini-deadline leading up to the due date.

Sample Output: *"**Project Timeline: Week 1** – Research and gather sources; **Week 2** – Draft outline; **Week 3** – Write first half of the paper; **Week 4** – Write second half and revise. Aim to finish initial research by [**date**], first draft by [**date**], etc."*

Tip: Use the suggested milestones to keep yourself accountable. If you miss one, ask ChatGPT how to adjust the timeline (*"I'm a week behind; how should I rearrange the remaining tasks?"*). Also, consider sharing specifics of the project (e.g., "*10-page paper on X*") for more tailored task breakdowns.

Intermediate 🟡

Prompt: *"I want to try time-blocking. Make a time-blocked daily schedule for tomorrow that includes: [**tasks to do**], meals, and short breaks."*

Use case: See your day mapped out with dedicated time slots for each activity, helping ensure you give enough time to each task and include breaks to recharge.

Sample Output: *"**Tomorrow's Time-Blocked Schedule: 7:00–7:30am** – Morning routine (**breakfast/get ready**) **7:30–9:00am** – **Task 1:** Finish English essay **9:00–9:15am** – Break (**stretch, grab a snack**) **9:15–10:45am** – **Task 2:** Math problem set... **8:00–9:00pm** – Relax/free time"*

Tip: Be sure to tell ChatGPT your waking hours or any fixed events (like class times) so it can schedule around them. Once you get the plan, try following it for a day. If a time block was too short or long, note it and ask ChatGPT how to adjust for a better fit next time.

Intermediate

Prompt: *"Something unexpected came up today, and I lost 2 hours. Help me adjust my schedule so I still finish my important tasks."*

Use case: Life happens! When you lose time to an interruption, use this prompt to re-prioritize and reshuffle your remaining tasks for the day or week.

Sample Output: *"Understood. Since you lost 2 hours, **let's trim or move some tasks:** Today, focus on [**most crucial task**] and [**second task**] only. Move [**less urgent task**] to tomorrow (**you have a free slot in the afternoon**). Also, shorten your study time for [**another task**] today from 2 hours to 1 hour by focusing on key problems."*

Tip: Mention which tasks can be shortened or delayed without major issues. ChatGPT's suggestion is a starting point—feel free to ask it to rebalance further if needed (e.g., *"If I do that, tomorrow becomes too full. Any other adjustment ideas?"*).

Intermediate

Prompt: *"Plan a 2-hour study session for [**subject**] using the Pomodoro Technique (**25 minutes study, 5 minutes break cycles**). Include what to focus on in each block."*

Use case: Get a structured plan for a focused study period with built-in short breaks, so you maintain productivity without burnout.

Sample Output: *"**2-Hour Pomodoro Plan for [Subject]:** - **0:00–0:25: Study [Topic A] (focus on [specific task])**. - **0:25–0:30: Break** – stretch, grab water. - **0:30–0:55: Study [Topic B] (work on [specific pages/problems])**. - **0:55–1:00: Break** – relax your mind. - **1:00–1:25: Review [Topic C]**... - **1:25–1:30: Break.** - **1:30–1:55: Quick recap of [Topics A, B, C] or practice quiz.** - **1:55–2:00: Reward yourself with a short rest!**"*

Tip: Treat the plan as if you had a real coach timing you. Set a timer for each interval. After the session, evaluate which blocks were most productive or if you needed more/less time on something, and tell ChatGPT for future adjustments (e.g., *"25 minutes wasn't enough for Topic B, how should I adjust the plan if I have another 30 minutes?"*).

Beginner

Prompt: *"I keep procrastinating on [**task**]. Break [**task**] into 3-5 tiny, actionable steps and suggest an easy way to start the first one."*

Use case: Overcome the inertia of a daunting task by turning it into bite-sized pieces. The key is that first tiny step that feels so easy you can't not do it.

Sample Output: *"**To tackle** [**task**]**:** 1. **Step 1:**... (**To start, just** [**super easy starting action**], **which should only take 5 minutes.**) 2. **Step 2:**... 3. **Step 3:**... Once you begin with Step 1, the rest will feel more manageable!"*

Tip: Actually do that very first tiny step as soon as you read it. Then come back and tell ChatGPT *"Done!"* – even though it won't know, this can mentally reinforce that you've started. If you still feel resistance, ask for an even smaller first step or some quick motivational words (you can even combine this with a Motivation prompt for a pep talk to get going).

Beginner

Prompt: *"I get distracted easily while studying. Give me 5 practical tips to avoid distractions and improve my focus during study sessions."*

Use case: Learn some straightforward techniques to stay on task (like turning off your phone, finding a quiet spot, etc.), coming straight from the AI as if it's your productivity coach.

Sample Output: *"**Tips to Stay Focused: 1. Create a distraction-free zone**: e.g., put your phone on silent and out of reach. **2. Use a timer:** set 20–30 minute focus periods (**knowing a break is coming can help you concentrate**). **3. Browser extensions:** if you study on your computer, use site blockers to avoid social media during study time. **4. Clear goals for each session:** decide what specific task to finish in the session. **5. Mini rewards:** promise yourself a small treat or a 5-min YouTube break after completing a chunk of work."*

Tip: Implement at least one tip immediately (for example, turn off notifications right now). You can also follow up with details about your environment (*"I study in my bedroom and my family is noisy"*) to get more tailored advice, or ask for strategies to handle a specific type of distraction.

Intermediate

Prompt: *"Design a daily routine for me that optimizes productivity. Include a focused morning routine, study/work blocks, and a relaxing evening wind-down."*

Use case: Establish a consistent daily rhythm that helps you start the day energized, get work done efficiently, and end the day calm and ready for rest.

Sample Output: *"**Ideal Daily Routine: Morning 7:00–8:00am:** Wake up, quick exercise or stretch, eat breakfast, and list top 3 priorities for the day. **Daytime: 8:30–10:30** – focused study/work block; **10:30–10:45** break; **10:45–12:00** – second work block; (**afternoon classes or tasks**)... **Evening 7:00–10:30pm:*** Dinner, *then free time or light review of the day's notes. **9:30pm** – shut off electronics, read or relax. **10:30 – bedtime.**"*

Tip: Be sure to mention any specific times you must include (like class schedule or work hours) so they fit into the routine. You can ask ChatGPT to adjust the routine to your natural habits (e.g., *"I'm a night owl"* or *"I feel freshest in the morning"*) to make it more personalized and realistic for you to follow.

Intermediate

Prompt: *"Help me balance my time. I'm a student with classes, a part-time job, and a sport. How can I allocate time to study, work, exercise, and rest each week without burning out?"*

Use case: Juggle multiple commitments by getting a macro-level plan that ensures you're not neglecting any area (academics, job, health, or rest). ChatGPT will try to distribute hours in a sustainable way.

Sample Output: *"**Weekly Time Balance Plan:** - **Classes: (listed times)** – focus on being fully present. - **Work: (listed times)** – use breaks there for light studying if possible. - **Sports practice: (listed times)** – counts as exercise and a break from academics. - **Study blocks:** Schedule 1–2 hours on free afternoons (**e.g., Tues/Thurs**) for homework/review; a longer block on Sunday for upcoming week prep. - **Rest:** Keep Friday evenings after 7pm free for relaxation or social time; aim for 8 hours of sleep nightly by setting a consistent bedtime."*

Tip: Communicate any signs of burnout or specific struggles to ChatGPT (like *"I'm exhausted by Friday"* or *"I have no time for friends"*). It can then adjust the balance, maybe by suggesting cutting back or rescheduling less critical activities. Always remember to include at least one full day or evening off in your schedule – ChatGPT can help identify where to fit that in.

Intermediate 🟡
Prompt: *"Using SMART goals, help me set one academic goal for this month and outline the steps to achieve it."*

Use case: Set a Specific, Measurable, Achievable, Relevant, Time-bound goal (SMART) – for example improving a grade or completing a project – and get a mini action plan to reach it.

Sample Output: *"**SMART Goal:** Raise my math grade from 75% to 85% by the end of this month. - **Specific:** Improve performance on weekly quizzes. - **Measurable:** Aim for at least 85% on each of the 4 quizzes this month. - **Achievable:** Current grade is 75%, will attend one extra help session per week. - **Relevant:** This will strengthen my foundation for final exams. - **Time-bound:*** 4 weeks. ***Action Steps:* 1)** *Schedule 2 hours each week for math review.* **2)** *Do 5 extra practice problems every practice session.* **3)** *Meet with the teacher on Mondays for clarification on last week's errors.* **4)** *Track quiz scores to ensure improvement."*

Tip: Once you have the goal and steps, put the plan into action immediately (e.g., put study sessions into your calendar). You can also ask ChatGPT to send motivational reminders or tips tied to this goal (combine with a Motivation prompt like daily tips to keep you on track).

Advanced 🔴
Prompt: *"Let me figure out where my time is going.* ***Yesterday I did the following: [describe your day's activities with times]****. Analyse this and tell me where I wasted time and how I can use those slots better."*

Use case: Perform a "*time audit*" with AI help. By sharing how you spent your time, you can uncover inefficiencies (like 2 hours lost to social media) and get suggestions on plugging those time leaks.

Sample Output: *"****Looking at your day:*** *You spent ~2 hours on YouTube/phone in the afternoon (****3–5pm****). That's a big chunk that could be partially redirected to homework. Also, there's a long gap between dinner and starting homework (****7–8pm****) where you felt 'tired'.* ***To use time better:*** *maybe take a shorter break after school (****30 min instead of 1 hour****) and start homework at 4pm. This would free up your evening. Also consider setting a YouTube timer for 30 mins so it doesn't eat up study time."*

Tip: Be honest and detailed with your described schedule for the best analysis. After ChatGPT's feedback, try implementing one change at a time (e.g., limit phone time in one specific hour) rather than overhauling your whole day. You can run another time audit in a week to see if the changes helped.

Intermediate

Prompt: *"I struggle to keep track of assignments and deadlines. What's a simple task management system I can use, and can you outline how I'd use it daily/weekly?"*

Use case: Get advice on a straightforward to-do list or planner system (digital or paper) and instructions on maintaining it, so you never forget an assignment or test date.

Sample Output: *"**Consider using a simple to-do list app or a planner:** - **Daily:** Each morning (**or the night before**), write down tasks and assignments for the day. Mark high priority items with a star. Check them off as you complete them. - **Weekly:** Every Sunday, list out deadlines and exams coming up that week. Break big tasks (**like a project**) into smaller tasks across the week. - **Capture new tasks immediately:** When a teacher assigns homework or a project, add it to your list or calendar right away with the due date. - **Review:** At the end of each day, review what's done and migrate anything unfinished to tomorrow's list. Also, peek at the next day's deadlines to prepare."*

Tip: Ask ChatGPT for specifics if you have a preference (e.g., *"How would I do this using Google Calendar?"* or *"Can this be done in a bullet journal style?"*). Once you pick a system, stick to it for at least a couple of weeks. You can even have ChatGPT act as a faux *"accountability partner"* by telling it what you plan for the week and having it *"check in"* (though that works best if you prompt it each time, see Motivation prompts for accountability ideas).

Intermediate

Prompt: *"Make sure I don't burn out. Given a busy week of classes and studying, suggest where to schedule some downtime or fun activities."*

Use case: Proactively include rest and recreation in your schedule – ChatGPT will look at a typical student week and pinpoint good times for breaks so you maintain your well-being and productivity.

Sample Output: *"**To avoid burnout, schedule short breaks daily and larger breaks weekly:** For example, take Friday evening completely off schoolwork to relax with friends or hobbies. Also, try to have at least one hour free each day for something you enjoy (**e.g., a walk, video games, reading for fun**) – maybe right after school before you start homework. On Sunday afternoon, after studying, reward yourself with a movie or outdoor time. These planned breaks will help you recharge."*

Tip: Share your actual schedule or the times you typically feel drained. ChatGPT can then be more precise (e.g., *"I often feel fried by Wednesday–where should I take a break?"*). Remember, downtime is as important as work time; if ChatGPT's plan feels too work-heavy, ask it to increase break durations or suggest relaxing activities that fit your interests.

Intermediate 🟡

Prompt: *"I want to build a habit of studying a bit every day instead of cramming. How can I start this habit and stick to it?"*

Use case: Get a plan for habit formation specifically for daily studying — including when to do it, how long, and how to keep yourself accountable until it becomes second nature.

Sample Output: *"**Habit Plan:** Start by choosing a consistent time slot each day (**e.g., 6–6:30pm right after dinner**) for dedicated study. Begin with just 20–30 minutes to make it easy to start. Set a daily reminder on your phone. For the first two weeks, stick to the same subject or a planned rotation (**Mon - math, Tue - history, etc.**) so you know exactly what to do. Keep a habit tracker and tick off each day you complete – seeing a streak can be motivating. If you miss a day, don't punish yourself; just resume the next day. After one month, studying at that time will start feeling automatic."*

Tip: Tell ChatGPT a bit about your day to find the best consistent time slot. If evenings don't work, maybe mornings or a free period can. You can also ask for motivational tips to pair with this habit (maybe combine with a Motivation prompt like a reward or a mantra). Over time, gradually increase the study session length or difficulty as the habit sticks.

Intermediate

Prompt: *"I have deadlines for assignments on [**date1**], [**date2**], and [**date3**]. How should I plan ahead so I'm not scrambling at the last minute for each?"*

Use case: Strategically plan your work on multiple assignments that overlap in timeline. ChatGPT will help stagger your efforts so you make progress on all of them without a last-minute pile-up.

Sample Output: *"Let's call your assignments A (**due** [**date1**]), B (**due** [**date2**]), C (**due** [**date3**]).* ***This week:*** *Focus on A first (**e.g., Mon-Wed:** research and outline for **A**; Thu: small tasks for **B** and **C** like choosing topics or gathering sources).* ***Next week:*** *Aim to have a draft of A done by mid-week, then switch to B – do major work for B Thursday-Saturday.* ***Following week:*** *A should be finished early (**buffer for proofreading before** [**date1**]). Use the freed time to concentrate on finishing B before [**date2**]. Start C in the gaps (**if C is later, even 30 minutes a day from now will help**).* ***Finally:*** *After B's deadline, you'll have [**remaining time**] for C – dedicate that entirely to C. Essentially, front-load work on the earliest deadlines but nibble on the later ones so nothing is left untouched."*

Tip: Adjust the plan as deadlines approach. If one task takes longer than expected, ask ChatGPT again how to recalibrate. Always leave a little buffer before each deadline for last-minute review. You can also specify the nature of each assignment (essay, project, presentation) and how heavy each is, so ChatGPT can prioritise accordingly.

Beginner

Prompt: *"I waste a lot of time on [**distraction, e.g. social media/gaming**]. Give me a strategy to limit this to a reasonable amount per day without cutting it out completely."*

Use case: If completely stopping your favourite time-waster isn't realistic, let ChatGPT suggest moderation techniques like time limits or reward systems so you can still enjoy it after important work is done.

Sample Output: *"To control [**distraction**] time, set a rule that you finish your priority tasks first, then enjoy [**distraction**] guilt-free as a reward. For example, allow yourself 30 minutes of gaming in the evening after you've done at least 2 hours of studying. Use apps or built-in phone settings to limit social media to, say, 1 hour a day – perhaps 30 minutes during lunch and 30 minutes in the evening. Also, try to keep your phone or game console out of sight during homework time (maybe in another room) so you're not tempted. By scheduling it, you'll still get to enjoy it, but it won't bleed into your study time."*

Tip: Be specific about how much time you think is *"reasonable"* or where your biggest temptation windows are (e.g., *"I always end up on YouTube after 10pm"*). ChatGPT can then tailor the strategy. You might also ask for a gentle reminder phrase or mantra to tell yourself when you're tempted, like *"earn your screen time"* – whatever helps reinforce the habit of finishing work first.

Advanced 🔴

Prompt: *"I'm leading a group project due in 4 weeks. Help me create a timeline assigning tasks to each team member, with check-in points each week so we stay on track."*

Use case: Manage a team project by clearly delineating who does what and by when. ChatGPT can propose a project management plan that you can share with your group to ensure accountability and steady progress.

Sample Output: *"**Group Project Timeline (4 Weeks):** - **Week 1:** Planning. **Tasks:** Alice – draft project outline by Wed; Bob – research background info by Fri; You – compile everyone's input and finalize outline by Sunday. (Check-in meeting on Fri to review outline and research). - **Week 2:** Initial Execution. **Tasks:** Alice – write Section 1; Bob – create visuals/data for Section 2; You – write Section 3. (Check-in on Wed to share progress, and Sun to merge sections draft.) - **Week 3: Refinement. Tasks:** Everyone – peer review another's section and suggest edits by Tue; Bob – integrate sections into one document by Thu; You – edit for consistency by Sat. (Check-in Thu after integration.) - **Week 4: Finalization. Tasks:** Alice – proofread entire project by Tue; You – make final edits by Thu; Bob – prepare the presentation by Fri.*

Tip: Adjust roles and timing based on your actual group members' strengths and schedules (tell ChatGPT if, for example, *"Alice is good at research, Bob at design"*). Once you have this plan, communicate it to your team and set those check-in meetings on everyone's calendar. You can even ask ChatGPT for advice on how to politely enforce deadlines with your peers if that's a concern.

Advanced 🔴

Prompt: *"Use the Eisenhower Matrix to sort my tasks into urgent vs. important. My tasks: [**list tasks**]. Tell me which I should do, schedule, delegate, or drop."*

Use case: Apply a popular time-management framework (Eisenhower's Urgent/Important matrix) to your task list. ChatGPT will categorize each task so you know what to tackle first and what can wait or be eliminated.

Sample Output: *"**Urgent & Important (Do First):** Task A (due tomorrow, important for grade), Task B (urgent health-related). **Important but Not Urgent (Schedule):** Task C (long-term project – plan parts of it over coming weeks), Task D (skill-building activity – schedule on weekend). **Urgent but Not Important (Delegate if possible):** Task E (club poster needed by Friday – perhaps ask a club member to help), Task F (household errand – maybe family can assist?). **Not Urgent & Not Important (Eliminate or do last):** Task G (binge new show – fun, but can be saved for when you have free time), Task H (organize old files – no immediate benefit, do later if ever)."*

Tip: You might not have someone to literally delegate to (especially for school tasks), but ChatGPT can still help you see what isn't worth your immediate attention. Use this categorization to focus your energy. If you disagree with a categorization, you can discuss why you think a certain task is more important and get ChatGPT's take – it might help clarify your own priorities. Over time, practicing this matrix with ChatGPT can train you to quickly prioritise mentally on your own.

Intermediate 🟡

Prompt: *"I tend to have energy peaks and slumps. How can I schedule my toughest study tasks for when I have the most energy? (I feel most alert during [**morning/afternoon/evening**] and sluggish around [**time**])."*

Use case: Align your schedule with your personal energy rhythms. ChatGPT will suggest when to do high-concentration work vs. easier tasks or breaks, based on when you feel most and least energetic.

Sample Output: *"Since you're most alert in the [**morning**] and hit a slump around [**3pm**], schedule challenging tasks (**like studying new material or solving hard problems**) in the mornings or right after your alert period starts. For example, do heavy studying from 9am to noon. Around 3pm when you're sluggish, **switch to lighter tasks:** review flashcards, organize notes, or take a short walk to recharge. Then, if you get a second wind in early evening, you can tackle another moderate study session. Essentially, protect your prime hours (**morning**) for the toughest work, and use low-energy times for easier or routine tasks (**or even a power nap if possible**)."*

Tip: Pay attention to your body's signals for a week and maybe keep a brief log of when you felt focused versus foggy. Share that info with ChatGPT (as you did in the prompt) for fine-tuned advice. Once you schedule according to energy levels, you should notice tasks feeling easier. If not, re-evaluate—maybe your peak times are different than you thought, and you can ask ChatGPT again with new observations (e.g., *"Actually, I felt super productive at 7pm—how to adjust my schedule around that?"*).

Part 3
Motivation

Use these prompts to boost your motivation, overcome study blues, and maintain a positive mindset through your academic journey.

Beginner 🟢

Prompt: *"I'm feeling unmotivated to study today. Can you give me a short pep talk like a coach hyping up their team before a game?"*

Use case: Get an instant injection of enthusiasm and confidence. ChatGPT will deliver an energetic, encouraging message to pump you up for your study session.

Sample Output: *"You've got this! Remember, all those small study sessions are adding up to something great. **Just like a coach says at halftime:** dig deep and give it your all! Even if you're tired, picture how awesome it'll feel to ace that test or confidently finish that homework. You've tackled challenges before and you came out on top – this is no different. Now take a deep breath, open those books, and show this material who's boss. I believe in you – let's go!!!"*

Tip: Actually stand up or change your posture while reading the pep talk – get into it as if you're about to charge onto a field. You can even ask for a specific style (like a calm encouragement vs. an intense rally) depending on what fires you up. Save particularly motivating messages to reread later when you need a boost.

Intermediate 🟡

Prompt: *"I failed an exam and it's really discouraging. Give me some encouraging words to help me bounce back and not lose confidence."*

Use case: Recover from setbacks with a gentle, confidence-restoring message. ChatGPT will provide empathy and motivation, emphasizing learning from the experience rather than dwelling on failure.

Sample Output: *"I'm sorry to hear about the exam – that feeling is tough, but please don't let it define you. Even the best students stumble sometimes. What matters is what you do next.* ***Think of this as a setup for a comeback:*** *now you know what to expect and what to focus on. Maybe you need a new study approach or just a bit more time on certain topics – and that's okay. You haven't come this far to only come this far. Pick your head up, take a short breather, and then let's make a simple plan to improve. You're smart and capable, and one test doesn't change that. In a year, this will just be a story about how you turned things around. You've got this!"*

Tip: **Use the encouragement to reflect positively:** you could follow up by asking ChatGPT to help you make a study plan to address what went wrong (combining Study Help + Motivation). Remember that it's normal to feel down – give yourself a treat or talk to someone supportive. You can even ask ChatGPT for a quick joke to lighten your mood after the pep talk!

Advanced 🔴

Prompt: *"I keep thinking, 'I'm just not good at this subject.' Help me reframe this negative thought into a positive, growth-focused mindset."*

Use case: Transform self-defeating thoughts into empowering ones. ChatGPT will act like a mindset coach, turning *"I can't"* into *"I can't yet, but I will"* and highlighting that ability can improve with effort.

Sample Output: *"Let's turn "I'm just not good at this" into something more hopeful.* ***How about:*** *"I'm not an expert at this yet, but I'm learning and improving."* **Or,** *"This subject is challenging, but with practice I can get better." Remember, every expert started as a beginner.* ***Instead of*** *"I'm not good,"* ***try thinking,*** *"What can I do to get better?" Maybe it's practicing 30 minutes more or asking for help on specific problems. You have to give yourself permission to be a work in progress. Each time you study, you're levelling up a little.* ***So swap*** *"I can't do this"* ***for*** *"I'm going to figure this out step by step." You'll be amazed what a difference that mindset shift makes!"*

Tip: Actually write down or repeat the new positive statement to yourself. You can ask ChatGPT for multiple alternatives and choose the one that resonates most. Consider putting the chosen mantra on a sticky note near your desk. Over time, whenever you catch yourself in negative self-talk, consciously replace it with your new growth mindset phrase.

Intermediate 🟡

Prompt: *"Tell me a quick success story of someone who struggled academically but eventually succeeded through perseverance."*

Use case: Get inspired by a relatable story. ChatGPT will summarize a real or fictional tale that shows how persistence can lead to improvement, making you feel *"If they did it, I can too."*

Sample Output: *"Sure!* ***Meet Alex:*** *In high school, Alex nearly failed algebra. He once got a 50% on a math test and felt completely defeated. Instead of giving up, he decided to stay after class twice a week for extra help and practiced a little bit each day. Progress was slow – his next test was still just a C. But he didn't quit. By the end of the semester, Alex scored an A- on the final exam! The same subject he struggled with became one of his strengths when he took it step by step. That experience taught him that hard work beats initial talent. Years later, Alex went on to use those math skills in his engineering degree. Whenever he faces a tough challenge now, he remembers how far he came in algebra. The lesson: struggling at first doesn't mean you'll struggle forever. Keep at it, and you can surprise yourself with what you achieve."*

Tip: You can specify if you want the story about a famous person (like *"Tell me about a famous scientist who failed something but succeeded later"*) or an anonymous student profile like above. Sometimes hearing about known figures (e.g., Einstein wasn't top of his class, or J.K. Rowling's rejections) can be very motivating. After hearing the story, visualize yourself as the protagonist of your own success story – what would that narrative sound like in a few years? Maybe ask ChatGPT to frame your situation as a success story from a future perspective for extra motivation.

Beginner 🟢

Prompt: *"I need a simple inspirational motto to keep me motivated during tough study sessions. Something I can repeat to myself."*

Use case: Have a short, punchy phrase you can recall when you're tired or frustrated, to boost your determination. ChatGPT will craft a slogan/mantra tailored to student life.

Sample Output: *"**Here's one:** "One page at a time, I'm building my future." It's a reminder that every little bit of studying you do is progress. **Or simply:** "Progress, not perfection." You can repeat either of those when the going gets tough!"*

Tip: Feel free to ask for a few options and pick your favourite. Once you have it, write it on a note and stick it on your study space or make it your phone wallpaper. Repeating it out loud a few times when you're hitting a wall can refocus your mind. If you ever get bored of it, ask ChatGPT for a new one or for the story behind a famous motto and why it's relevant (like *"Rome wasn't built in a day"* or *"No pain, no gain"*) to keep it fresh in your mind.

Intermediate

Prompt: *"I find [**task**] super boring. Can you gamify it or turn it into a fun challenge to help motivate me to do it?"*

Use case: Make a dull task more engaging by introducing game elements or a sense of competition. ChatGPT will come up with a way to challenge yourself or add points/rewards to the task.

Sample Output: *"Absolutely! Let's turn [**task**] into a game. For example, if it's reading a textbook chapter, give yourself 10 points for each section you finish. Set a timer and see how many points you can rack up in 30 minutes. Or, create a bingo card of things to find/learn in your notes – each time you identify one, cross it off. If you get a bingo, treat yourself to something nice! Another idea: pretend you're racing a "boss level" - you have to answer a question correctly at the end of each page to move on. Keep track of streaks and try to beat your streak each time. Turning tasks into mini-competitions with yourself can make it much more fun. Ready, set, go earn those points!"*

Tip: Actually keep score or records of your game if applicable. You can also involve friends: for example, both you and a classmate set the same challenge and then compare who *"won"* (who got more points or finished faster). If one method doesn't make the task fun enough, ask ChatGPT for a different angle (like incorporating a storyline or characters, if you enjoy role-playing, e.g., *"You are a wizard and each math problem solved is a spell cast"*). It might feel silly, but if it keeps you engaged, it's worth it!

Intermediate 🟡

Prompt: *"**Help me visualize my success:** describe what it will feel like at the end of the semester when I've accomplished my goals, to motivate me now."*

Use case: Stay motivated by picturing the satisfying payoff of your hard work. ChatGPT will paint a vivid, positive scene of your future success that you can keep in mind when you're grinding through work.

Sample Output: *"Imagine it's the last day of the semester. You walk out of your final exam and let out a deep breath – you did it. Remember how anxious you felt months ago? Now you're smiling because all those study sessions paid off. You check your grades later and see the improvement you were aiming for: that tough subject you worried about is now a victory, maybe even with a comment from your teacher like "Great job, well done!" You feel proud, not just because of the grade, but because you proved to yourself you could do it. You're more confident signing up for next semester's classes. And best of all, you can start your break feeling free – no lingering regret, just well-earned relaxation. That sense of relief and accomplishment is amazing. Hold onto that feeling during each study session now – it's what you're working toward!"*

Tip: Close your eyes and really absorb the scene described. Athletes use visualization to gear up for success; you can too. You might ask ChatGPT to focus on particular details that motivate you personally (like imagining telling your family about your success, or how you'll reward yourself, etc.). Re-read this visualization whenever you're in a slump to remind you of the "why" behind your efforts.

Intermediate

Prompt: *"I'm really anxious about an upcoming exam. Can you guide me through a quick calming visualization or breathing exercise to reduce my stress and boost my confidence?"*

Use case: Calm your nerves and get in the right headspace before a test or presentation. ChatGPT will walk you through a short mindfulness exercise combined with positive reinforcement.

Sample Output: *"Okay, let's try this. First, sit comfortably and close your eyes. Take a deep breath in through your nose... and slowly exhale through your mouth. (**Do this three times.**) Now, picture yourself walking into the exam room feeling calm. You sit down, read the first question, and **you realise:** you know this! As you breathe, imagine a gentle wave of relaxation flowing from the top of your head down to your toes, releasing the tension. Any time a nervous thought pops up, acknowledge it and let it drift away like a leaf on a stream. You are prepared. You've studied, and you know more than you think. Envision writing your answers confidently, and then see yourself handing in the paper with a small smile, knowing you did your best. Take one more deep breath... and open your eyes. You've got this, and you are calm and ready."*

Tip: Actually follow along with the exercise as you read it. You can ask for a specific technique if you know one that works for you (e.g., *"Can you do a 4-7-8 breathing guide?"* or *"Help me do a body scan relaxation."*). Before the real exam or stressful event, consider quickly re-reading this or even having ChatGPT send a last-minute reminder like *"You're going to do great!"* as a confidence booster.

Advanced ●

Prompt: *"Give me a 7-day motivation plan. For each of the next 7 days, provide a short encouraging message or tip to keep me on track with my study goals."*

Use case: Receive a week's worth of daily motivation upfront. ChatGPT will output seven mini pep talks or tips, one for each day, almost like a motivational calendar.

Sample Output: *"**Day 1: "Kickstart Monday:** Set a small goal for today and crush it. Every big success is just a series of little wins – go get one now!" **Day 2: "Tuesday Triumph:** Remember why you started. Each hour you study today is a step closer to your dream. Keep that momentum!" **Day 3: "Wednesday Wisdom:** Midweek check-in: reward yourself for how far you've come (**even if it's just a little treat after finishing that chapter**). You're doing great!" **Day 4: "Thursday Thrive:** If you feel tired today, do just 15 minutes – often that's enough to get in the zone. You've got the discipline, trust yourself." **Day 5: "Friday Finish Strong:** End the week proud. Push a bit today so you can relax this weekend knowing you earned it. Future you is already thanking present you." **Day 6: "Saturday Steady:** It's the weekend, but a short review now will save you stress later. Then enjoy your day – balance is key!" **Day 7: "Sunday Refocus:** Take a moment to reflect on all you achieved this week. Even setbacks teach lessons. Plan out next week's goals, knowing you can handle anything it brings."*

Tip: Consider setting these as reminders on your phone for each morning or writing them on your planner for each day. If a particular day's message doesn't resonate, ask ChatGPT to tweak it (*"Can I get a more energetic message for Wednesday?"* or *"I usually rest Sunday, can you make Sunday's message about recharging?"*). This way, the motivation plan truly fits your routine.

Intermediate

Prompt: *"I want a few positive affirmations to boost my confidence as a student. Could you give me 3 affirmations I can say each morning?"*

Use case: Start your day with self-affirming statements that reinforce your abilities and potential. ChatGPT will provide a handful of *"I am..."* or *"I can..."* statements to build your confidence.

Sample Output: *"**Sure! Here are three affirmations: 1.** "I am capable of learning anything I put my mind to." **2.** "I deserve success because I work hard and I believe in myself." **3.** "Every challenge I overcome makes me a stronger, smarter student." Repeat these to yourself in the morning or whenever you need a confidence boost!"*

Tip: Tailor the affirmations to areas you struggle with. If self-doubt is your issue, ones like above are good. If procrastination is an issue, something like *"I take charge of my time and make the most of my day"* could help. Feel free to ask ChatGPT for replacements or more options. Write them on a card by your bed or say them in the mirror. It might feel odd at first, but affirmations can set a positive tone for the day. Stick with them for a while; consistency is what makes them sink in.

Intermediate

Prompt: *"I'm losing sight of why I'm studying so hard. Can you remind me in an inspiring way why education and learning are worth it for me?"*

Use case: Reignite your intrinsic motivation by understanding the value of your efforts. ChatGPT will craft a motivational reminder of how education benefits you and aligns with your goals/dreams.

Sample Output: *"**Think about what education really is:** it's your ticket to opportunities. Every hour you spend hitting the books is an investment in you – your future career, your personal growth, your ability to understand the world. It's worth it because it builds confidence; remember the thrill when a tricky concept finally clicks? That's you growing. Also, your hard work now might mean landing that dream job later, or being able to help others with the knowledge you gain. And beyond jobs, learning enriches your life – it makes conversations deeper, decisions smarter, and you become a more independent thinker. You're not just memorizing facts; you're training your mind to solve problems and chase dreams. So when you're asking "why," know that it's because you have a bright future that you're preparing for. Education is the bridge to get you there, and you're building that bridge brick by brick. Keep going – future you is already proud."*

Tip: Reflect on your personal reasons (like a career goal, a person you want to make proud, or a dream lifestyle). You can share those with ChatGPT so it can tailor the message (*"I want to be a doctor"* or *"No one in my family has gone to college before"*) – it will likely incorporate that into an inspiring reminder. Save this response and read it whenever you ask yourself *"What's the point?"*.

Intermediate 🟡

Prompt: *"Give me a fun, humorous motivational message to make me smile but also encourage me to get back to work."*

Use case: A light-hearted pick-me-up that both amuses you and gently nudges you to stay on task. ChatGPT will combine humour with motivation (perhaps a witty analogy or a playful tone).

Sample Output: *"Study Palooza Time! Okay, break's over – the books miss you. Remember, if you get your work done now, you can party with Netflix guilt-free later. Your assignments are like clingy pets: they won't leave until you feed them attention. So give that problem set some love! You've fought tougher bosses in video games than this math homework, so I'm 100% sure you can conquer it. Future You is doing a happy dance because you're about to crush it. Now go show that homework who's the boss, champ!"*

Tip: Think about what kind of humour makes you smile – maybe self-deprecating, maybe memes, maybe super corny dad jokes – and ask for that style (*"make it meme-worthy"* or *"include a pun about science"* etc.). You could even have ChatGPT craft a funny short song or rhyme if that brightens your mood. Laughter releases tension, so once you're smiling, it should feel easier to dive back into work. If this works for you, consider scheduling a *"humour break"* every so often where you get a quick funny motivational hit before continuing your study session.

Beginner 🟢

Prompt: *"I want to reward myself for studying hard. Suggest a small reward I can give myself after I finish [**task**], and hype it up so I stay motivated."*

Use case: Positive reinforcement! ChatGPT will recommend a treat or break and then talk it up enticingly, so you have something to look forward to as you grind through the task.

Sample Output: *"Finish [**task**], then it's reward time! How about [**reward**, e.g., **a cup of your favourite hot chocolate and an episode of that show you love**]? Imagine curling up in your chair, wrapping your hands around that warm mug, and taking that first sweet sip, thinking "Ahh, I earned this." You'll enjoy the show so much more knowing your work is done. It'll be the perfect relaxing treat after all that brainwork. Just picture it: task done, worries gone, and you in full cosy relaxation mode. Keep that in mind during the last stretch of studying – every bit of focus now gets you closer to that yummy, well-deserved break!"*

Tip: Pick a reward that genuinely makes you happy (doesn't have to be food or TV; it could be playing 15 minutes of a game, a quick chat with a friend, a walk outside, etc.). You can ask ChatGPT to suggest non-food rewards or rewards that don't cost money if you like. The key is that the reward is reserved for after you finish the task – and by having ChatGPT vividly describe it, you turn it into a motivational carrot dangling in front of you. If you find yourself slipping, remind yourself of the reward waiting for you. After completing the task, as you enjoy the reward, acknowledge to yourself *"I earned this."* This builds a positive study-reward loop.

Intermediate 🟡

Prompt: *"I often procrastinate because I'm a perfectionist and fear my work won't be good enough. Encourage me to start anyway and not worry about being perfect."*

Use case: Get over the paralysis that comes from wanting things to be perfect. ChatGPT will give you a compassionate shove to just begin, emphasizing progress over perfection and that mistakes are okay.

Sample Output: *"It's totally understandable – you set high standards for yourself. But here's a secret: even a "B+" start is better than an "A+" plan that never happens. If you don't start, you can't improve it. Try telling yourself the first draft (**or attempt**) is just for your eyes only and it can be as rough as it needs to be. You can always polish later. In fact, some of the best projects/start-ups/essays began as messy first versions. Progress beats perfection, every time. You'll likely find once you begin, the work will evolve and get better naturally. And guess what – even if it's not perfect, it can still be really good! Remember, done is better than perfect because done means you're moving forward. So give yourself permission to be imperfect and just dive in, you might be surprised at how well it turns out."*

Tip: Set a very small initial goal, like *"I'll work on this for just 10 minutes,"* to trick your perfectionist brain into allowing a start. **You can even ask ChatGPT:** *"Remind me that my first draft doesn't have to be perfect in a funny way"* to lighten the mood. Sometimes reading quotes from famous creators about imperfection helps (e.g., the quote *"Perfect is the enemy of good"*). You could ask for one of those too. Ultimately, remember you can't edit or improve a blank page – so any start is a win.

Beginner 🟢
Prompt: *"Mornings are tough. Can you give me a motivational 'good morning' message to help me get out of bed and ready to tackle my classes?"*

Use case: Wake up on the right side of the bed with an upbeat greeting. ChatGPT will provide a friendly, positive message that makes you feel excited (or at least less grudging) about the day's opportunities.

Sample Output: *"Good morning! Time to rise and shine! Think of today as a new page in your story. You've got your plan, your goals, and a whole day to make something great happen – even if it's just learning one new thing in class or sharing a laugh with a friend. Your breakfast is waiting, the world is waking up with you, and guess what? You're going to do awesome things today. So, take a deep breath of that morning air and let's get this day started! You got this, and I'm cheering you on. Now go show Thursday who's boss!"*

Tip: Set this up as part of your morning routine. You can actually have ChatGPT (if using an app or shortcut) give you a fresh message each day. Or simply save a particularly motivating one and read it first thing. Pair it with an energetic action – like stretching or playing a favorite song. If there's something you usually look forward to (even if it's just a good cup of coffee or a chat with a friend at lunch), remind yourself of that in the morning message. You can ask ChatGPT to incorporate such details (*"Mention that I get to play basketball after class, which I love"*). Over time, a positive morning mindset can make a big difference in motivation throughout the day.

Advanced 🔴

Prompt: *"I have trouble holding myself accountable. Propose a strategy I can use to keep myself accountable to my study schedule, and motivate me to actually implement it."*

Use case: Get a concrete accountability method (like a study buddy system, a reward/penalty system, or tracking chart) and some motivational persuasion on why and how to follow through with it.

Sample Output: *"**One strategy:** The Accountability Checklist + Buddy System. First, create a simple checklist of your study tasks for each day (can be on paper or a notes app). Each night, tick off what you did. Next, find a friend or family member and tell them your goals for the week. Ask if you can send them a brief update each evening ("Studied math 1h, read 10 pages for English"). Knowing someone expects that message can really push you to avoid the "eh, I'll skip it" trap. Even pretending you have to "report" to someone (**like writing a journal entry as if to an audience**) can work. Now, **here's why to do it:** when you hold yourself accountable, you're basically proving to yourself that your word matters. It's building self-trust. The more you check off or report "I did it," the more confident and motivated you'll feel."*

Tip: Actually create that system right after reading the advice. If it's a checklist, make it for today and tomorrow. If it's a friend, send that text invite now. Sometimes just taking that first step in an accountability system is the hardest; once it's in place, it can carry you. You can ask ChatGPT for other strategies if this one doesn't appeal (like *"What if I used rewards/penalties?"*). Also, make sure to choose an accountability partner who is positive and supportive if you use one.

Intermediate 🟡

Prompt: *"I feel like I haven't made any progress lately. Give me a motivational message that points out that small steps count and I'm probably doing better than I think."*

Use case: Combat the feeling of stagnation by highlighting that improvement often happens gradually and that you likely have grown (even if it's not obvious to you). ChatGPT will encourage you to recognize incremental progress.

Sample Output: *"It's easy to miss progress when it's happening bit by bit. Think of it like growing taller – you don't notice it daily, but then one day your clothes fit differently. Every study session, every homework problem, every page you read is a small step forward. Maybe last month you didn't understand a certain chapter and now it clicks - that's progress! Trust that all these small victories (like that slightly better quiz score, or recalling something faster than before) are adding up. You are definitely doing better than you think. Keep stacking those bricks one by one, and soon you'll step back and realize you've built a solid wall of knowledge."*

Tip: Try to list a couple of tangible improvements you recall (no matter how small). If you can't think of any, ask ChatGPT to help identify some typical subtle signs of progress in learning (like improved recall, slightly less time needed on tasks, etc.). Sometimes tracking your work (like journaling study hours or using an app) can give you data to see progress (e.g., *"studied 5 hours this week vs 3 hours last week"*). Combining motivation with data can reassure you that you're moving forward. And yes, celebrate even the tiny wins – they keep you going for the big ones!

Intermediate

Prompt: *"When I have a million things to do, I freeze up. Can you encourage me to take it one step at a time and not get overwhelmed by the big picture?"*

Use case: Overcome overwhelm by focusing on the next actionable step. ChatGPT will coax you into a calmer state of mind, emphasizing that you only need to handle tasks one by one, not all at once.

Sample Output: *"I hear you – having a huge to-do list can feel paralysing. But here's a comforting truth: you can only do one thing at a time, and that's completely okay. You don't have to climb the whole mountain today; just focus on the next step in front of you. Pick one small task – maybe the easiest or the most urgent – and start there. Give it your attention, and ignore the rest for the moment. Once that one is done, you'll feel a bit lighter and more capable. Then move to the next. Each tiny step forward is progress. You might even find that momentum builds and your stress eases as you knock tasks out one by one."*

Tip: Physically write down your tasks in a list if you haven't, then literally cover everything except the one task you're working on (use a sheet of paper to hide the rest or fold the list). This visual focus reinforces doing one thing at a time. You can ask ChatGPT for help prioritizing if you're not sure which task to do first (connect with a Time Management prompt perhaps). After completing a task, give yourself a tiny mental high-five or mini-break, then address the next.

Intermediate

Prompt: *"I often hesitate to ask for help when I'm stuck because I feel shy or dumb. Motivate me to seek help (**from teachers or friends**) when I need it, and remind me it's a smart thing to do."*

Use case: Reduce the stigma or fear around asking questions. ChatGPT will encourage you by explaining that seeking help is a sign of strength and will ultimately benefit you, not something to be ashamed of.

Sample Output: *"**Remember:** asking for help is part of the learning process – even geniuses ask questions! It doesn't mean you're dumb; it means you're engaged and care enough to understand. Think of it this way: if something is taking you 3 hours to figure out alone, a quick question to a teacher or friend could solve it in 10 minutes. That's smart and efficient. Teachers actually appreciate when students ask questions, because it shows you're trying. And your classmates? They've probably had similar doubts and might be relieved you brought it up. Everyone needs help sometimes; nobody gets through school (**or life**) completely solo. So next time you're stuck, remind yourself: asking for help is a shortcut to learning. It's brave and proactive, not weak."*

Tip: **Challenge yourself:** ask at least one question this week, whether in class, via email, or to a friend. Start with something small if you're very shy. Notice the response – it's likely positive or at least neutral. Each time will build confidence that nothing bad happens when you ask for help. You can even share with ChatGPT the outcome (*"I asked and it wasn't so bad!"* for a virtual high-five). Also, keep in mind others often respect those who seek clarity; it shows you're responsible about your learning.

Intermediate 🟡

Prompt: *"Studying can be so boring for me. Could you suggest one or two creative ways to make studying [**subject**] more fun and motivating?"*

Use case: Find enjoyment in the learning process by switching up your study methods. ChatGPT will propose creative strategies tailored to the subject, like turning it into a game, using multimedia, or integrating your hobbies.

Sample Output: *"Sure! Studying [**subject**] doesn't have to mean just reading the textbook. **Here are a couple of ideas:** - **Gamify it:** Try using quiz apps or flashcard games to test yourself. For example, for history dates, pretend you're on a game show and "buzz in" (**even if you're alone**) with answers. Give yourself points and small rewards for getting questions right. - **Teach it to a friend (or pet!):** Explaining concepts out loud in your own words can be surprisingly fun. Grab a family member, friend, or even line up your stuffed animals and teach [**subject**] to them, complete with silly examples or drawings. You'll find yourself more engaged and might even laugh at how you simplify things. - **Mix media:** Tired of the textbook? Look up a catchy YouTube video or song about the topic (**there are math concept songs, historical event raps, etc.**)."*

Tip: Pick one suggestion and try it during your next study session. If it's a flop (not every method works for everyone), try the other or ask ChatGPT for more ideas (*"Any ideas specifically involving music? Or involving movement since I like to move?"*). Sometimes combining with your interests helps (e.g., if you like drama, act out a historical event; if you like tech, turn notes into a slideshow with fun graphics).

Bonus: Prompt Power-Ups

Want to go beyond the basics? Here are three advanced ways to stretch your prompts and get even more out of ChatGPT:

Combine Prompts:
Use two prompts back-to-back for compound tasks. For example, use a Study Help prompt to summarise a concept, then follow up with a Writing prompt to draft a short explanation or essay. You'll get clearer, more in-depth answers that suit your assignment needs.

Rephrase for Tone & Style:
ChatGPT adapts to tone, format and intention. After your first response, try asking:

- *"Now rewrite this in a persuasive tone,"*
- *"Make it sound more academic," or*
- *"Turn this into dot-point notes."*

This is perfect for creating multiple formats from one idea – like revising essays, emails, or presentations.

Prompt Stacking:

- Use a series of prompts to layer understanding. For example:
- Start by asking for a summary
- Then request a quiz on the content
- Finally, ask it to generate flashcards or real-world examples

This technique is ideal for exam prep, deep dives, or mastering difficult topics.

About This Guide

ChatGPT Catalyst: Student Edition was created to help students learn faster, write more clearly, and use artificial intelligence with confidence. Every prompt in this book was chosen to solve a real-world challenge — from time management and motivation to essay writing and revision planning.

This guide isn't just a prompt list. It's a toolkit designed to work with how you think and study — whether you're juggling work, college, university, or high school. It's been built to remove the friction and decision fatigue that often comes with learning or writing under pressure.

AI isn't a shortcut. But when used well, it's an amplifier — helping you do more of what matters in less time. Our goal is to give you the right inputs so you get the best outputs, without the guesswork.

What's Next

This is just the beginning.

We're already working on future editions of ChatGPT Catalyst, including:

- Academic Writing Edition
- Sharpen your voice, polish your arguments, and structure essays like a pro
- TAFE & Uni Study Skills Edition
- For vocational and tertiary students managing practical workloads and theory-heavy content
- Personal Productivity Edition
- Learn how to plan better, stay focused, and use ChatGPT to manage your energy and time

To access updates, resources, or new releases, visit our website or follow our store pages on Gumroad, Etsy, and Amazon KDP. You'll also find printable worksheets, companion videos, and advanced prompt sets launching soon.
This is your launchpad. The deeper you go, the more value you'll unlock.

COREPRINT

Legal Note

This publication is intended for general educational use and is not affiliated with, endorsed by, or sponsored by OpenAI or its partners.

All content, prompts, structures, and suggestions have been developed independently to support student learning. While care has been taken to ensure relevance and accuracy, readers are responsible for how they apply this material in academic or professional settings.

ChatGPT outputs can vary based on user input, platform updates, and context. Always verify facts, ensure originality where required, and follow your school or institution's academic integrity guidelines. CorePrint accepts no liability for how this material is interpreted or used.

Made in the USA
Las Vegas, NV
17 October 2025

32481393R00055